Pursuit of a Wound

Pursuit of a Wound

Poems by
SYDNEY LEA

University of Illinois Press
Urbana and Chicago

Manufactured in the United States of America

♾ This book is printed on acid-free paper.

Library of Congress Cataloging-in-Publication Data

Lea, Sydney, 1942–

Pursuit of a wound : poems / by Sydney Lea.

p.   cm.

ISBN 0-252-02577-6 (alk. paper)

ISBN 0-252-06817-3 (pbk. : alk. paper)

I. Title.

PS3562.E16P87   2000

811'.54—dc21   99-006987

1 2 3 4 5 C P 5 4 3 2 1

Digitally reprinted from the first paperback printing

For my mother, Jane,
my mother-in-law, Marty,
and my friend, Larry Lieberman:
the nurturers

Acknowledgments

The author expresses his gratitude to the editors of the following magazines, who originally published the following poems, sometimes in slightly different form:

American Scholar:	"It Has Orange Teeth"
Ascent:	"English as a Second Language," "Retreat"
Connecticut Review:	"Local Story: Reading the Signs," "Poor Fool Blues"
Dark Horse:	"Ars Longa, Vita Brevis,"
	"Girls in Their Upstairs Windows,"
	"Publishing Project," "Pursuit of a Wound"
Georgia Review:	"The Drift," "Fin de Siècle,"
	"October Incident, 1998"
Gray's Sporting Journal:	"Well, Everything"
Hudson Review:	"After Valentine's," "Authority," "Ballad,"
	"Reasons to Hate Poetry," "Yoked Together"
Kenyon Review:	"Conspiracy Theory,"
	"Inviting the Moose: A Vision"
New Yorker:	"November"
Quarterly West:	"For Such Reasons Do I Write Another Letter"
Southern Review:	"Champlain: West Shore: Cartesian"

"Inviting the Moose: A Vision," "Yoked Together," and "Well, Everything" appeared in *New England Poetry: An Anthology,* ed. Robert Pack and Jay Parini (Hanover: University Press of New England, 1999).

Contents

Pursuit of a Wound

—Buonconvento, 1997

I've forgotten the name of the family in Torre Gentile who owned that sickened ewe, her every part scrawny, but for her udder, which bag was so enlarged that she kicked and trampled upon it whenever she moved. Which happily wasn't often. *La poverina:* so the daughter, Serena, would constantly murmur, without once being moved, however, to soften the pain or put the poor beast away. She might survive after all; it wouldn't do to euthanize. Why do I call this up from these decades back, from another part of Italy from this one, where—the power failing in a storm—I feed our daughter Cheerios for comfort? Milk runs down her breast, a candle flame quavers. Each neighbor at Torre Gentile: *simpatico.* My new wife proved daily such an unmerited wonder that the town's very vine and earth and stucco and stone seemed to have flown my way out of old romance. And yet for all of that, that savaged ewe suggested each disorder the planet had known. In each of the teats' abrasions I imagined her bleat of pain gone general, and in her gaze, every living being's brutish confusion. The dam's last lambs were long since butchered, quartered. How little it took to turn me sentimental. How little it takes me still. I am so little, drab tourist here in the land of noble Dante. Today, in the vines, I saw a clutch of pheasants, the mother hen flopping from me as if—wounded. As if I'd pursue a wound. Which of course I did. Then morning slithered to *sera* and on into *buio.* The rain arrives at an end abrupt as its start. Candle fire stands upright, and our small girl's eyes catch, break its light into stars. I love her, love her, bundle her close. She'll suffer, die, like me. A nightingale sounds, and earth becomes what it is, or ever was. Which for this moment seems all it needs to be.

Part 1

Reasons to
Hate Poetry

Yoked Together

The warden, cop, and vet all told me on the phone the coon must be destroyed,
provided, like them, I possessed the means to do it, as for better or worse I did.

He'd come up out of our woods and onto the porch and simply would not scare.
He had stuff running out of his eyes and skinny, tatterdemalion hair

and he probably had, therefore, rabies. Or maybe distemper. In any event,
surely something was wrong, and according to the doctor, my good friend,

something abnormal enough it likely posed a not inconsiderable health threat
to our family, our dogs, our property, and to other families and to other pets

and also to what he called "the wildlife community." By the time I got done
searching for keys for the gun cabinet, he stood out there in the winter garden,

where now and then he pawed at the wilted greens of a buried carrot, pausing
now and then as well to lift one foot, and next the other, and looking

more than anything bewildered. He reminded me of poor gone Arthur,
the idiot from one town away: he and I used to split up wood together,

and he'd sort of do the same thing with his legs, and his eyes were also ringed
with black. (He smoked a filthy corncob pipe, through which everything

must pass: milkweed, leaves of grass, cigars, cigarettes, chew—you name it.)
I suppose I thought of him because he too was above all else bewildered.

He'd squint and scratch his head, as if he never completely understood
—no more, really, come to think of it after all these years, than I could—

why I'd show up at his shack every late August with the saw rig and the maul
to help him fill his woodshed, which was no more than an empty pony stall.

I imagined using, precisely, a maul on this poor, disheveled, sickly beast
because I didn't want my small daughters to hear me fire the shotgun blast

that would do him in. Yet I admit I was also afraid to get too close,
and I likewise must have supposed a bludgeoning would make an awful mess,

and somehow it might have felt too much as though I'd brought a heavy blade
down on baffled Arthur, the coon's human image, as I've already said.

The shotgun having been fired, the creature fell and huffed once. Then: silence.
And I, no more than a dreary man of letters, as if my knee had jerked,

thought of myself at one end and Arthur at the other of a cropped white birch
and of a famous poet's phrase about things being "yoked together by violence."

The Green Room

In Key West, our world spilled gleaming quarters. 1962.
My friend Bart and I would ram the coins
into the stand-up jukebox of the billiard parlor, in series,
paying off bets to each other, choosing that one tune again and again:
Hey, hey-hey, baby, / I wanna know if you'll be my girl.
Why did the Green Room, beneath the slow
teak ceiling fans that wheezed and whirled
and barely ruffled the napkins under our Cuba Libres,

while we played our dopey song and our one-pocket pool—
why did it seem an erotic Eden? Foolish, yes, though we were nobody's fools.
Or so we had thought, hustling our way southward, bar to bar,
until we hit Hilliard at the Georgia border, where we lost the whole bundle
to a courtly Greek who played us for the chumps we were.
I wince now at our posturing, our swagger,
our rehearsed, fake-Kerouac road life. Two pampered collegians. I shudder.
And yet to have once been so young is forgivable,

I hope, to have once been so stupid. I accused Bart
of staying that way after graduation, working for some bloated reactionary
congressman from Nowhere, Missouri.
I remember charging him on the same count with "having no heart."
I turned out in the end to be right, if not in the way I thought.
We quarreled, we lost touch, and today comes word of his coronary.
No wife or child survives him. So I guess it's *nada;* goose egg; zip; naught.
In that spring in the Green Room, however,

chastened though we'd been by the skillful Mediterranean,
and thus now inclined to play with no one except each other,
the world felt plentiful, the world was all before us.
(He or I may actually—Lord!—have quoted that line from Milton
in *Paradise Lost*). We'd surely find some women. Just now hitting our strides,
we'd surely shortly marry, procreate. And yet we'd still sing above the chorus
of humans who merely, drearily lived, and ate, and worked, and died.
We'd go on forever singing to the very world:

    Hey-hey, baby, will you be my girl?

After Valentine's

—for Tink Hood, a reader

I snowshoed back by evening of Valentine's Day, or one day past.
So call it late afternoon.
I upbraided myself, who've remained in all these fifty-odd years on earth
so damnably slow to notice things, important or otherwise.

Hiking, for instance, I'd somehow recognized the absence
from my northcountry woods of the logging ramps,
themselves constructed of logs
back in the days of timber horse and handsaw.

Decades ago, they had already started to crumble,
heart-leaf popple trees grown up within their grids;
but now they've simply moldered down to mulch and loam,
though I hadn't considered them gone till today.

Just so, in other places, the Milky Way is no more,
nor the forest edge, all quick with game,
nor the resonance of names.
Unbinding the shoes, I whispered *Union Street Bridge,*

words that once suggested trout and ephemerid,
and even before I made for it quickened my pulse and my breathing,
as I imagined casting a line
downstream from this nineties sprawl of stores and fern-clogged bars,

the valley now become what's called by travel agents and tourists
a "destination"—as surely it was for me back then.
But that was different: I was a child,
I must have reckoned

that naming an object of love could hold it forever.
That love was destiny.
And now my mind keeps turning, turning,
its trail as blurred as my snowshoes'.

I drive with care, for instance, because my daughter, eighteen,
yesterday flipped a car on Interstate 91.
Today she might be gone,
I might be broken to pieces,

I might be whispering *Erika, Erika,* over and over again,
aloud, and cursing all this waste, this ruin.
I might be longing to bring back horses.
Instead I'm merely making my way back home.

I've bought some staples—milk and eggs—at the store.
The time of the horses was hard, no doubt,
I mustn't sentimentalize.
And yet there's the sick blue glow in so many windows, from television,

and the church bell hasn't even chimed out six.
The log ramps pointed toward the Connecticut River:
knowing this (or knowing stars), you could find your bearings
if you were lost. I heard as much from my neighbor Tink,

whose profile I see through his living room window.
Backlit by lamp glow, he's reading, as ever, his favorite.
Or not his favorite, really. Rather his one-and-only.
"By God, if once you try him, you'll never read no one but Louis L'Amour."

Or so he's told me.
Tink was a roofer. Now, at seventy-four, he refinishes yard sale chairs and tables
and coddles the creatures of his domain:
each fall he conspires with the chickadees that hop up on his palm

beside his handmade feeder,
with squirrels that scoot through his shop all winter.
He reads. He laughs.
The shop is full of gimcrack junk he buys for a joke:

the moose horn toilet paper rack, the cow flop telephone,
the Cupid denture holder,
and that big plaster of Paris dog, a St. Bernard,
around whose neck he once arranged a collar,

its outsized tag reading SYDNEY LEA.
Reading Lea: now that's a thing that Tink will never do.
Don't we deserve that, we cynical poets, our hearts not in it,
who form a guild, and nothing nobler, and vanish?

Tink, I say, as planets orbit, as brook ice jingles, as a gravid deer appears.
Tink, I repeat, as if I were raising a glass.
And why in the end not offer a toast to Louis L'Amour,
if only because his name means love at last?

For Such Reasons Do I Write Another Letter

—for Dianne Pearce

Because she could, without stencil, with the commonest paring knife, fashion these semiperfect stars in the dull clay of this plaque she gave me; because at six years old she could adjust the oven just so, with authority; because she knew without a glance at any clock exactly when the glaze set; because her little artifact does appear childlike in its mild asymmetries and for the same reason melancholically adult; because I remember her hands as square, blunt, despite the bony, the angular look of her; because but for avuncular love I had and have no claim upon her; because she would read (at six!) anything from the most banal of boardbooks, *Spot, Shapes,* to complex novels and read them twice and more; because I myself now read this tablet twice and more, and read all these things about her up from the terra cotta, and want them stored; because I want the weight of these hollow figures lodged in the pocket nearest my heart; because I want never therefore to change my foul shirt; because I witlessly vow not to change it till someone does it for me, till I too am crossed by whatever it is (not likely—he was so old—the oversized car driven by the undersized, confused man who couldn't see her on her bicycle, who could scarcely make out the road); because I want equally to imagine these stars as evil and to cast them therefore into some bottomless salt cove:

For such reasons do I now in tears undo everything, and especially everything I've written up till now, or even known; and then do I write to my friend, her mother, another letter: a letter useless and tepid as any bad poem.

English as a Second Language

The professor of American Literature finds himself in Buda in springtime.

He strolls along the great street Vilányi, whose bordering chestnuts upthrust
their white cones of petal, quick wind clearing the air at last, dachshunds
yipping and komondors glowering out from grillwork yard enclosures.
Small traffic. No human sound. He's alone, though not especially lonesome.

At Moricz Square, Vilányi meets Béla Bartók, smaller, more subtle.
A tram stops here and flower stalls crowd each other and the open market
thrives and countrywomen sell lace and fruit and produce by the blacktop
and teenage girls wear the tightest clothes imaginable. He pauses, ponders,

as though taking notes (which he does, if only inside his head). A tourist—
why not acknowledge as much? How else would he speak of himself anyhow?
Magyar won't be learned. A folk art store is chockablock
with tile and stag horn gewgaw. The same drunk snoozes by the spirit shop:

will he never wake up among the heaped flasks of cheap *barack* around him?
Sunday is quiet here in town, under the famous Buda hills.
A federal building in Oklahoma has just been blown from existence.
In a cart over there, one monstrous onion. Again our literature-lover

stops. The onion. The chestnut blossoms. The vendors' daffodils.
All . . . explosive, he mutters, then smiles, then feels his heart drop gutward,
sensible as he is of sin in this matter of language and letters,
which turns everything to delusive coherence. *Syntax sucks.* He envisions

that slogan scrawled on a bathroom wall . . . by him, by the visiting scholar.
Then a band of gypsies (is that truly the best he can do, "a band of gypsies"?):
out of an alley they pour (likewise), in pursuit of a pair of grim,
shrouded wives. They are . . . hopping mad. That phrase seems somehow
                                                                    fresher,
since in fact he's never before seen a person hopping in anger.
These women do, while cohorts encircle their battle, which breaks the silence.
He's lost in cliché. What tongue do they speak? It can't be Hungarian, can it?
Or not for the most part, although he does recognize "my husband"—*a férjem*

—and hears *tolvaj*. (It'll be hours till he can look up that one: "thief.")
Snickers and hoots resound as if from a schoolyard. Our professor is looking
on from a distance. At equal distance two skinheads loll against trees;
he is glad they don't seem to pay much mind. This scene: there is humor in it,

but something, he feels, isn't funny at all. Something, he feels, flies in
on late-April whispers of breeze. The small tram, departing, rattles, stammers.
The women freeze in their tracks, fall silent, bolt. The bleary drunk rises
and stumbles away. Then all are running away. The professor must flee,

though everyone's impulse shrouds itself in unspeakable mystery.

Publishing Project

It was a great idea, so sure, of course, I volunteered to type
for the local fourth graders, who wanted to "publish" a book of their stories;
I myself had been publishing stuff for years, but my early attempts
still somehow felt important, even if glory

didn't attend them (and hasn't elsewhere since, I moped in self-pity): *Jeep*
was one of my earliest magazines; and *Creative Moment;* and *The Lamp
and the Rabbit*. (Say what?)
But after a while, as I sat at the keyboard, I felt trapped

in some pop culture dream, where everything had to do
with Power Rangers, Nintendo, and *boom* and *zap* and *budda-budda-budda*.
Where, I wondered, did imagination ever go?
Or so remained my attitude till one narrative came along, in which, rather

than reciting the struggles, lapses, and recoveries
of superheroes, the author provided an antiheroic account
that rang too unhappily true. "Too true
a tear" it almost evoked, to quote the seventeenth-century poet Vaughan. (Who?)

It was one of those same-old-same-old stories of discovery,
although the heroine didn't seem to know what she'd actually found.
(The fiction, clearly, was no fiction.) It involved a wedding,
at which, she said, *Daddy kept shouting and laughing also dancing*

and Mommy me and Tiffny however didn't dance with no one not once
She spoke briefly too of the moon, but more tenderly of standing by a fence
behind the groom's trailer, which, unlike her own (*on good days*),
was not *kept neat,* and of how *there was a pony out there*

it was between a brown and a bay
(she knew horses, I guess) *and acted better than where it come from*
there was so much whiskie and smoke the pony smelt better than the air
and it was a dirty rotten shame to leave him and a shame

me Mom and Tiff had to go home with Uncle Ware
which wasnt ever that nice to us and isnt an uncle but Mom says hes a friend
and look!! This is supposed to be a story of one of the good days
and look how it ends up just like this PS

by Tami THE END

Reasons to Hate Poetry

at least sometimes: as when little Jimmy, four years old,
whose smile can take the temperature of winter rooms
—softwood boughs heavy with soot-dirty snow outside, and the sky
a tin cup's color, rat-tatting walls with something between snow and rain:
can take their temperature and then, shining, jimmy it up, up . . .

as when, I was saying before, he flies
out through the misted back window of the beat, Bondo-patched Ford,
of which, in a hurry for school and work, his mother has lost control, and which
pursues its awful arc till the trunk end whacks an ash
and the tag sale car seat's cheap catch quits, as quick as my dead dad's World

War buddies said Italians would. I hate a lot of poems because I'm rich
compared to Jimmy, or at least that's part of what I despise, and the poor kid's
head finds that very tree, oblate leaves sprawled corpselike on the ground,
and deeper in woods, one imagines the chant of an owl,
though it be daytime. I'll somehow suit its eight interrogations to the scene,

which is all a palimpsest of ruin, is all a stillness now—no, is panic and wound
and that spooky call, which, however, I've had to invent, this being a poem,
whose prospects I loathe enough that it can't really seem to start.
Hence irrelevant allusions to war; my gone father; his gone friends;
Italians; "palimpsest"; corpses. Hence the goddamned owl.

But a poet, he takes or makes all this to show his largeness of heart
(or sometimes hers, though perhaps less often, granted).

Our sensitive poet puts Jim in a nearby clinic, a tangle of I.V. tubes
in his body, sedated because it gets violent because he's got no notion of Fate,
is not like us—o childhood! o innocence! And though we won't say it,

a part of us breathes: a poem! a poem! There's so much with nothing to do
with him that we can include. In his mother, who has bad teeth
and a waitress job, we may see a recapitulation, say, of Mary-who-mourns-
her-Son, savaged. We can shout our indignation at power,
American power, which reviles the weak. We'll write such a powerful poem.

The helicopter, air ambulance that drones
above, will present a figure. For something. We'll dream it up later.
Meanwhile, we could use another bird: let's look one up in a book
to be sure it lives here and so may seem true; it will perch on a strand
of wire by a fallow farm, which that 'copter can fly, heedlessly, over.

We need the harshest song. (Oh, what we'd do for a rook!)
The wail of despair, cruelty, poverty, the wide world's wealth of wrong.
"Middle East" will always mean turmoil: example. Guns. Bombs. Knives.
Most whites, if not us, oppress everyone and -thing we might think to name
with might. But we can't go on. Or not I, rather. Not here, thank God,

thank Fate, whatever. Jimmy survives, and the smile that shines. He's alive.

Part 2
Local Story

November

Mack's insides still ached from the test
at the fancy new clinic. The pain bothered less, though,
than how he'd had to lie there like that—Lord!—rear up,
and even the nurses watching. Almost to home now,

he saw Riddle's herd, the lot of them lying down on the ground.
Everything pretty and sad: the Holsteins'
black and white that bold and true, and after a rain-day or two,
the grass—more than in summer—that green.

The mountainsides showed their trees shaved clean,
except for the dark of the oak and the beech leaves, over the river,
fog on the bald ridges awful, the white of ice. Already.
Not cancer.

He ought to be relieved, said the doctors.
They only found some little thumbs—a five-dollar word he forgot
the minute they named it—on the bowel wall.
Not uncommon, they called it. Like death, Mack thought.

He passed the school. Everyone up on the swings or on foot:
Tag. Football. Capture the flag. The kids
still looked like October in all their bright clothes.
They raced as if wind-chased, fast as he drove. So this wasn't it.

Not the six dragged-out months that his young wife got,
and not a shock, either, like their one child Thelma's accident.
He was all right, but he'd die.
You know that the whole while, but then one day it's different,

like going by Fifth Mile Meadow and now there's a house built in it,
or a restaurant you dress up for where Joey Binder's mill was.
Mack determined not to get going on that. Not again.
He'd turn up his hill, check his mailbox,

maybe come back and *fix* the foolish mailbox,
about to lie down on its side. He'd check in on his tiny string
of heifers. Instead he held steady, north.
Watson claimed he'd got out of dairy for good, just barbering

full-time in his little shop in the yellow frame building
across from the feed store: it hadn't changed much, if at all.
"Say that for the rest," Mack whispered. "Say that."
And their talk hadn't changed. Animals, crops. But before Watson could pull

the paper ring from around his neck, Mack spoke: "Well,
I'll have a shave." How did it happen? It felt like dreaming.
"Yes, I guess I'll have a shave," he decided.
And then, the cloth on his face steaming

while his friend gripped the ivory handle in his big fingers, stropping
the blade on dirt-dark leather, Mack said
through the fog, "I haven't had this done in years. Years."
But it felt good. Lord, it did feel good!

The Drift

And ay the ner he was the more he brende.
For ay the ner the fir, the hotter is . . .
   —Troilus and Criseyde

With each ground-eating stride he keened, *Mama, Mama, Mama.* Poor Freddy
Dunbar, whose type not I nor town nor nation shall see again: the Village Fool.
He came back daily, even at eighty, to the cellar hole, still plumb, still sound,
though full of vines and ember dust from the day the house burned down.
Now, among these sour soils and long-cool coals, the sightless moles are adrift.

Here I am on the river, here in my raft. Last night a fire engulfed a local man,
up at Ryegate Corners. In his truck, beside a road made treacherous by rain,
he slept off things. But his cigarette still glowed and his rusted can of gasoline
waited behind the seat like Satan. Likely the tin boat on his trailer showed
a life's sad icons: a few perch flopping, gasping in the hull's rainbowed water;

a doughnut box; a Boone's Farm Country Cooler; scattered tickets of no worth
for the lottery. For all I see, as I watch out for rocks, there might not be
another soul on earth. I prophesy in hindsight as I cast my streamer fly along
the bends. Nothing will rise. Only my foolish recall of Freddy—long stride,
topcoat in all weather, copper skin. (It's yet believed that his mother's mother

was a slave.) I spied on him one day, creeping cross-lots through the woods
to watch him squat and rock. He mumbled *Mama* beside that sunken frame
of granite. I'm ashamed.
                     Ours: the age of e-mail. Speed is all. I can't not feel it.
My mind's the slave. Speed, terror blend: I think of TWA Flight 800—New York

to Paris. I tumble down this faster Middle Fork; divers probe those other depths.
I can't and don't control my own progress. Shocked by sun, riffles and slicks

assume some molten metal's hue. There was a village boy; he died last month in a wreck. His parents' lawn stays so richly bleak—so eloquently unmowed. On Independence Day, now thirty-odd years ago, a car mowed Freddy down.

All seems collision and conflagration. Air takes on its chill of autumn, and yet my oars are dark with my own sweat. I've loved how rapids bring the world close and make me briefly see it, sane. For now that world accelerates to flame: the Dunbar shack reduced in seconds to cinders in that cellar hole; a horde of murderous automobiles; this hot-steel surface; that plunging plane.

Inviting the Moose: A Vision

Sumac thickets by the roadbed, either side,
spangled by snow and the big moon's light.
Deeper in, evergreens, taller, darker,
but still undark in that light, this weather.
And deeper yet, hardwoods that scatter and climb
    up Signal Mountain, which I climb down in a car, toward home.
    A saxophone keens on the tape machine—slow, sweet
    balladry, which seems just right.
I whisper, "What a night."

Twenty minutes east, my twelve-year-old son
composes a story in his upstairs room.
His two younger sisters are breathing, way down in slumber.
Downstairs, my wife eases split remnant lumber
into the stove for kindling
    and then—nothing grave—she goes on thinking.
    In mind and fact, the world appears
    intact, to me at least, who am torn between here
and there, to me who fear

one set of pleasures may cancel another.
It's like the dilemma of any lover,
craving anticipation and, equally, consummation.
But who'd complain at such benign frustration?
Everything glows. The wayside drifts, for all their sand and salt,
    are gorgeous as they descend, like the fault-

less bassward glissando of the horn
as I glide by Kettle Pond.
Whenever the season is warm,

its open water invites the moose of our region.
And I? I summon a vision.
My knowledge, for all my years, remains slight:
Why, I wonder, tonight of all nights,
should I invite the moose as well?
 Antlerless in late winter, the bull
 precipitously vaults the righthand guardrail
 and comes to a standstill
before my automobile.

One of the daughters shifts in dream. Rolls over. Smiles.
My son's narrative, meanwhile,
proposes at its climax that goodness is a sword.
The saxophone and the sidemen find their resolving chord.
All might end right now, right here.
 My wife muses by her warming fire.
 There's no moose, of course, just hallucination,
 on no particular occasion,
on a flank of Signal Mountain.

 No moose at all. Just strange desire.

Poor Fool Blues

After he hanged himself at twenty-two,
the town got together and planted a tree in his name.
Breck's tree. Rock maple. It would be stalwart and good
in time, this sapling. We meant it to have a meaning—
though what sort, exactly, none of us could say.

Today, April Fool's, I visited on my way home,
the first small wisps of leaf just bursting the buds,
the root-knees straining for purchase in loosening earth.
Rain came down on me, stiff, and kept the kids
inside the school where Breck himself was a boy.

Nothing let itself be understood,
articulated, though everything seemed so common, so plain.
Root. Leaf. Rock. Mud. Wind.
These weren't booze. These weren't crack or horse,
nor the cheap leather belt he fashioned into a noose.

There's likewise now an art award in his name.
On driving away, the very first thing I saw
was a bumper sticker: LIFE'S A BITCH AND THEN
YOU DIE. There's more to it than that, I sighed,
countercliché my pathetic recourse.

I wheeled along and shivered, wet to the core.
But off to my east, above the Connecticut

River by Big Pat's farm, where he keeps those burros—
small muscular demons, sad-eyed—a squadron
of geese, the first of spring, headed north.

Do I turn off Buddy Guy, I idly thought,
on my radio shouting, "The first time I met the blues
they followed me tree to tree," to hear a chorus
of honks so familiar and strange they might be arranged
in 4/4 time as well, twelve bars, three chords?

I told myself, *Either way you can't lose.*
The music's changes still thrilled, like geese in the sky,
who drag a heartbreak past and a hope to our doors.
We fools keep on. We look for meaning and form.
If patterns and breaches of pattern wear out our words,

we still mean to do some good before we die.

Retreat

Because a Manhattan friend once wrote me that my North "seems at times like a retreat," and I then burned too many hours pondering that, and do still; because, fine, there exist more interesting, crucial things in this world than I, such as, just for example, that skin-and-bones washed up in the January flood in a town south of here the other week—concerning which the authorities say there's no reason to suspect foul play, and say it as if foulness were other than a fact of life; because my mind has played back such a matter, and will. Or: because, as I prose on in a poem, gnatty morons clutch their cellular phones in some so-called gentlemen's club, and watch some so-called exotic dancer,

stretch marks hidden under her short "schoolgirl's" outfit, thinking she shakes "just for them" (oh America, where are we going, for God's sake?), fantasizing a sexier call than they'll ever get; because in parentheses like the preceding, as my good wife tells me, I'm at my most importunate; because the snow, yet falling outside, seems ready to go on till the end of earth, with its homicide on the fortunate and unfortunate alike, especially unfortunate, especially south; Or: because there was a schoolmarm in my earlier life—I can say *schoolmarm,* you see, I'm old enough now—whose assignment for each of us was to write to a soldier, a "serviceman," as she put it, there being few military women then,

WACs, or valiant, unheralded nurses (you see, this really was long ago). I offered my correspondent a hypothesis: "It must be exciting in Korea." By which I meant to show: Life in these fifties was too dull, tranquil. It was, too, although our class wag, Leo, one weekend, when we broke into school and felt thrilled to be there voluntarily, found—hidden amid the shambles of that very teacher's top drawer—a certain medal (though we made nothing

of that, our irony still rudimentary). Because he didn't write back, that grunt:
because all these things apply,
and because there is therefore no reason in this world why I
should attend so to the workings of this fetid little mind of mine, but do,
here on Vermont Route 132:

because of all this, I confess
I'm more than a little embarrassed now to scrutinize the simple fact—
which somehow I find . . . interesting—that I have just now changed my radio
from NPR's *La Traviata* to local country/western and Travis Tritt, whose song
about foolish pride I treasure. What-oh-what does it all mean? Nothing,
except that, all along, anyone's life is, more or less, one foot in front of the other
. . . till something with luck arrives and helps us to find in the forth-and-back

an order, to help us imagine that imagination can deal with what I attest
to imperfectly, can make a link between such x-y-z and, say, this other thing
that as I drive occurs to me: I mean the burning chicks, their nest
ablaze each spring in the chimney, the mother always flown, when we opened
Daddy's camp, back then when he was alive. Why did she always return—
come back and back? Now, as if anyone but I and my family were concerned,
I retreat north up Vermont 5, happy enough myself to live, though it'll be
twenty miles before they stop their rattle in my car, my head: the tiny, charred
claws, bones, light almost as the very air, flooded in unconscionable prolixity

on the hearth, seeming too trivial and slight even to think of as dead.

Well, Everything

After the cancer got down in his bones, poor Bill
didn't want much to kill—not even on the wing.
Still, he did have that crackerjack young gun dog Belle,
just now getting round to her best, her prime-years savvy.

Wouldn't she be the wrong damned creature ever to waste?
Then Joey, of course. The kid. Yes, Joey, too.
(Forty-something, he was by now: "The kid," by Christ!
but there *is* a whole lot of difference: forty and sixty.)

He'd take them out, he would, old Bill McCrae.
The birds were scarce, they were wicked scarce, compared,
even in the county's last cover lasting a day.
Then came the end of that day, the end of that season,

when you saw those cones, foot-long, all bluey-violet.
Toward night they jump right out from your shotgun's barrels.
Near dark, but by Jesus, Belle pointed and held it solid.
It seemed like a gift, to someone, the way things happened,

because up flew not just one, but two big grouse
(or "brace" as his late true-Scot Uncle Belding put it,
pretending to be old school or something high class,
instead of some stiff, like any McCrae, some millhand).

Joe pulled on the left-barrel trigger, straightaway
(at least the boy still uses a side-by-side,
not like those city nuts from the NRA,
the ones that call themselves "ballistics experts").

You talk about expert! Belle held. She held, by God.
Joe missed his bird, no matter he's made of himself
a pretty fine shot. Belle held. Bill whispered, *Well, good.*
The kid dropped the harder one of the pair in the dirt.

And Bill, he said it again, *Well, good.* You see:
It came to him right then that everyone here
that wasn't dead as that bird was more or less happy
here at the close. And thinking so seemed to bring

to Bill a familiar but kind of a far-off commotion:
he thought, *All this is just like going through
any sort of repeated, well-known motion.*
Then, goddamn-it-all, as if it had wings,

the christly Crab flew right back into his mind.
It's been a good life, he reckoned. Oh yes, more or less . . .
(Here Baby! Here Belle! Here Darlin'! Here Sweetheart! Here Child!)
So what was so different now? *Well, everything.*

Hearing Test

My hearing is ruins. It garbles my brainways enough that I question now, again, for the thousandth time, if I can believe it: Did the radio newsman really just report the charge against the three boys from one county north?

They actually stabbed to death an aged dairy couple's cow? Knifed her freshened heifer, who aborted her first calf? True serial killing, if so. Or so I imagine. My tinnitus prompted the past hour's test: these ears, especially

the right, unclinically, ring. They can often incline me to oddest misprisions, which sometimes make me laugh: I listened, for instance, once to a student of mine as he told another, "Yes, in fact, I have a William Faulkner necktie."

How did the garment *look?* I wondered. Dark, I guessed. Densely patterned. Uncommonly long. I knew and liked the young man, so couldn't keep from asking what in fact he'd really meant to say. So when I mentioned Faulkner

and his necktie, he giggled like the kid that, fifty-odd myself, I thought him to be. "I said," he corrected, "I have my Williams seminar today." For me, thank God, I had some sense of humor left: I roared. But when *I* was a kid,

all Sundays brought abscess and nightly aching to that right ear. My mother, awakened, would fill a thimble with gin, pour it into that red canal to stop the throb. I woke, myself, to ropey saliva that tangled my tongue. Off then to Dr. Hitschler, who lanced that weekly chancre. Years later, he'd make me sit with pieces of metal stuck up each nostril. Radioactive, stainless-steel rods. My sense of smell is therefore of course a ruins as well.

Bored all those hours, I skimmed the *Geographic*. Now some expert "counselor" gibbers on air. He says, "American children are bored today. That's a fact; we might as well know it."—Or at least I imagine he says so,

over the radio's static. The hospital—new, splendidly exurban—looks like an airline terminal. And will those boys ever know in their lives for sure the impulse that moved them to murder? More important, will they care?

There seemed small hope, the audiologist acknowledged: My sort of loss doesn't do well with hearing aids. She was young, pretty, congenial, sweetly spared time to explain what the test had been all about. There was

first that series, fading to nothing, of beeps and of moans: some were keen, some dull. (The latter sounded like *moos,* I think, though I'm sure that this is now a fancy of mine.) Every time I heard one, I had to push the button.

Then she asked me if I could distinguish among some words she whispered —especially if I could choose among the revealing consonants. "Try to say *kill,*" she ordered. "Say *pain.* Say *will.* Say *feel.* Say *brain.* Say quickly,

truant-ruminant-ruin." Then she pointed out the places where I had failed.

Local Story: Reading the Signs

Perhaps she has time to mutter, "I'm not drowning,"
because she's heard the claim that—when you are—
your life's events replay themselves in a rush.

Like this, most likely, she reasons: it seems an hour
between the start of the skid and the dive into brush,
a dog-hair thicket of it, September turning

the leaves to tourists' colors there on the shoulder.
She thinks about her only child, who was born
when Dawna herself was a baby, and now how grandmom

is probably watching the poor kid watching the reruns
there in the trailer. Dawna remembers its knickknacks:
a violet herd of tiny porcelain deer

grazing on smoke; clay choirs of angels, who tune
their harps, while Disney's dwarves stare at the door,
as if their princess soon might enter the room.

That isn't brush, after all, but a deep, deep stack
of poplar trees. She whispers, *Billy sucks,*
and even imagines painting such a thing

on the bridge that lay ahead. (His nickname was "King.")
She did get those fourteen months with AmeriCorps,
where the counselors taught her how to set an alarm,

how to punch in, and what a condom was for—
as if she didn't know. But what the hell . . .
The King, she's heard, is out in Butte, Montana.

She recalls the spell she worked on that Kansas farm
(on payday, she'd hang around at Destiny Lounge,
her baby left home; she knows that was wrong); and then a

three-month bartending gig on Oahu, until—
well, she just flat couldn't stand it any more:
you needed some seasons, some snow, some colors that change,

your daughter. Her car slow-motions down the hill,
so the whack she gives the first of those gilded popples
feels much too hard, like the time Bill ran them ashore

too fast in the boat, though they thought at the time they were able-
bodied, not stoned or drunk; they heard the curses
—"Drown, you fools!"—from the lakeside picnic tables.

When the rescuers find her, two cops, two techs, two nurses,
she's already sunk. Yet I've pieced out a reasonable story
(I'd bet) from details in her three-inch obituary.

It Has Orange Teeth

—after a story told me by the late Lesley Childs

He made it a habit to cast his *dorothea*
—each night, all that June long—to one trophy trout,
whose skepticism cured Lesley of being a dreamer
for the moment; that was what fishing a fly was about,

he told me: the world come down to pure concentration.
You saw the rise, you threw a line above it,
no further thought entered—not self, not family, not nation.
You were both away and clearheaded. That's why he loved it,

remotely, like loving your way through a tumble of water,
mindful only of boulders and eddies, the rest,
the universe, having shrunk. There was only disaster
if he let his mind or canoe go anywhere else.

He said that he timed false casts to his quick breath's rhythm,
then dropped the dun on the slick, while overhead bats
and swallows were hunting, although he didn't see them.
(Everything superficial, I punned.)
                                        The slap

behind him felt something, therefore, akin to the blow
a sheriff once fetched him. The cop suspected narcosis,
not his first *grand mal*. What oddly had seemed like a flow
in his life—a current bound to draw him the closest

he'd ever get to a kind of blessed distraction—
turned into a mangle of strobe light, obscenity, threat.
That night it was only a beaver, whose own concentration
lay in getting her way to the west, to her twig-hungry kits.

Bank beavers, he said, whose home "weren't no more than a hole
in the high-rolling tier by the rapids," which Lesley at last
was compelled to notice. Cliché came to serve him: "My soul,"
he said, "was all nightmares: present, future, and past,

"and each ran into the other, and each of them nameless."
The beaver's a creature so placid you might call her staid.
In fable, she represents the virtue of habits,
but her warning caused Lesley to hear rebukes from the dead

for spending his time in trying to obliterate time;
he'd spent too much at conniving to get himself laid
or at trout or at poker, nights when he should have been home,
too much in indifference, his wife lying cancerous in bed.

Les reeled, then stuck his fly in the rod grip's cork.
The beaver pounded again, then glided cross-river.
Dizzy, he feared a seizure there in the dark
for the first time in years. Had he taken the pills? He shivered.

After that evening, he never again went out wading.
It seemed hard enough to get through a day on dry land.
He never made out what the river ghosts had been saying.
Yet they had addressed him, he knew. And a terror remained.

October Incident, 1998

Rich and I were playing at disappointment:
the goddam Yankees were going to the series again
and the stupid Sox about to lose Mo Vaughan.
We stopped at the diner there on old Route 10,

just minding our beeswax. "Goddam! I want hash *browns!*"
So this sucker said, as Jenny milked the urn
of coffee for one of a hundred October clients
and answered: "We got home fries and no hash browns."

Sucker stood there and countered her at her counter:
"I *need* hash browns." Well, Jenny's just as tough
as she is sweet, like the truck stop's hotcakes. He
was working his way to the tough side. She went gruff:

"If there's a problem, take it upstairs. Us girls,
we only work here." The moron sported an earring,
an almost transparent goat beard, and a still
store-creased work shirt—but he was spoiling,

it looked to me, for a fight. So I—old
but as ever big—I stood up too. I snapped,
"Shut your face or get it out of here."
"Hash browns," he said. A whisper. The place was mobbed

with tourists—who'd blame them?—who mob Vermont
this time of year to see the foliage, which
showed dull this fall, compared to some. And me?
I was just looking forward to a hunt with my old pal Rich,

"Hash browns," the guy insisted, no matter what.
Through the window behind him Blue Mountain, whitened with sun.
Jenny calmed. She patted my forearm. She poured
this nut more coffee, for free. I knew her son

had died in '97 on I-91,
when a drunk went wrongway up a ramp. Well,
each of us has troubles. "All I needed
was just . . . hash browns," he stuttered. "Just them, was all."

That dumb-ass earring was something I could've ripped
right off his face. Thank God I didn't. The beard
looked the same as mine did, back in my teens.
The guy wasn't evil or drunk. No, only weird,

obsessive. I'd scared him. He was less unruly now,
plaintive and smaller. Rich, hours later, would comment
on the morning's ceaseless overflights of geese:
"Listen to them; a new wedge every minute."

The wildfowl sounded like all we two could need.

Pumpkins: Late September

Thousands of pumpkins in Wally Morse's fields, brighter
than this so-called peak foliage,
eastside-westside, down by the river.

The tourist bus unloads. I wish I knew how to take pictures
myself. I don't even own a camera.
I might take snapshots of pumpkins and seven Mexican laborers

in Wally's fields in this crispest autumn sun,
harvest time down by the river in old Vermont,
which must look about like the moon

to the Mexicans, who are here because . . . Can you say needy?
Send the fuckin' check south. Do the fuckin' math.
Frost will be here, as ever, before we can say "Speedy

Gonzalez." *Buenas tardes,*
I say and say to one worker after the other: each,
for reasons of survival, dallies,

moves without speed. *¡Oye! Cockfight tonight.* The days, though—
they're getting shorter.
Still, I have plenty of time to love those folks,

without any earthly reason.
He, Speedy Gonzalez, was that old cartoon mouse—
like me, I think somehow, in the perishing season,

lucky rich mousy mixed-tongue bastard though I be.
I forgot my happy pill
this morning, so no wonder... But let's see:

Everything's looking gorgeous, at its peak—
so say the lying Greyhounds—but everything seems also sad.
In Québec City, just north, last week

I checked out this *images méxicaines* exhibit at *le musée
de la civilisation*. Civilization. Sure. ¡Oye!
Signs claimed that the Mexican sensibility "says nay"—

elle dit non—to death as finale. We won't really be gone.
(Rough translation.) Sure. The pumpkins will die soon, unless . . .
Your author speaks several tongues,

but—beyond "good afternoon"
and assorted irrelevant
phrases—not theirs, not yours. Gone soon,

pumpkins, Mexicans. Wally's just trying to make a living.
Aren't we all? Whom, if anyone, am I forgiving?

Part 3
Fin de Siècle

Conspiracy Theory

Through that Taft Hotel window, the local radio station's neonized call letters
over the New Haven Green
now had the alien look of shimmery desert, deep space, one's oddest dream.
First National's carillon was tolling again,
no longer timely, bullets long since cold in the famous cadaver. Those bells

sounded ugly, more so than ever. Elitists all, we'd come to Yale but inhaled
this murdered Harvardian's meritocratic notions: you could get smart
but have a decent conscience, we thought, could study Locke, Bach, Chaucer
—and later be a Freedom Rider.
Everything, we tried to believe in our hearts, would work itself out in the end.

I didn't recognize it then, but this person had been my only
female friend who *was* pure friend, and nothing besides.
We'd hug and weep and sigh, talk out our own inadequacies, hopes.
And that was that. We were, I suppose, merely lonely.
She must have been no wiser than I, must have known no better what we had.

How but in such ignorance could we two have made our way to bed?
It was an old nexus, sex and death. And faced with this *thing* in Texas,
this sundering of our faith, however callow,
why shouldn't we be irrational too? But now I wonder why we couldn't value
our never having done what then we did—so pitiable, feckless. Don't ask me.

It was the last place for us, bed. We would never return to where we'd been,
not entirely. We just couldn't do that, before she did herself in.

Not suicide, exactly, but not exactly not: she starved herself to death.
By which I don't suggest, or imagine, she did so because of what we'd done,
just before Thanksgiving vacation: crudely, badly done.

A labor it was, of hours, which stopped at last for no reason, except our lust
to stop at last. After which those radio letters, the mumbling walkers below,
the looming Sterling Library towers: each had an off-putting radium glow.
The world felt new, strange, worse, even our conversation
leaping off the point completely,

whatever the point may have been. Our talk turned terse, uncustomary.
For all our so-called education, we didn't have a clue.
Advisors were working in Indochina now, but that wasn't in any course.
A group of Englishmen—across the sea, in some German cellar,
their hair absurd (by the times' standards)—

were ripping off black American rhythms and playing their same three chords
again and again, behind banal words: "I Wanna Hold Your Hand." "Love Me Do."
There lived a sad-sack fellow, James Earl Ray, whom nobody knew.
And I might have noticed, but somehow didn't, the yellow
cast to my woman friend's cheeks or her ribs, which if not yet quite Biafran—

another name we didn't yet speak—were on their way. She ate only aspirin.
Against the smogged night, her profile showed translucent as the drapes.
Her end, I guess, was also on its way: like Watergate, Sirhan, Cambodia, AIDS,
Ali uncrowned by cretins. *Conspiracy* became a watchword, and is so today,
though it means a breathing together, as if women and men

could draw a common air, which was precisely what it seemed back there
no two of them would ever—ever—really do again.

Our Camp, '63

—in mem. B. R.

"Say what's the matter with our camp?" "Our camp's all right!"
"Well, who say so?" "Well, we say so!"
Then the chorus: "Everybody—everybody!—love the Advocate

Camp, Advocate Camp!" We'd chant slowly, then faster, faster, and at the close
Joyce Dutson and Thelma Tewkes and Caroline (last name for now forgotten),
huffapuffing, laid their bodies down

at Eighteenth and Diamond, where my late brother and I (oh yes, she was
                                                                    Johnson)
worked at the Church of the Advocate and were in every way stoned
on the innocent earlier sixties stuff like Sam Cooke's "Bring It on Home to Me,"

or the fucked-up notion that a summer church day camp allowed
us to do something to help a nation in its narcosis rectify
the deaths, countless, in bilge-watery choleric slave ships and what followed

and follows and then we'd all be fine. As we boys just hung out, they danced,
these tiny lovely terrific girls, as I doubt even the famous Russians—
Nijinsky-Nureyev-Baryshnikov—could do. They'd do, say, a hand prance

over the unforgiving jump rope's repetitions
or do things blindfolded or one-legged. You'd barely believe what you saw.
Where are they now, sweet children, who had never heard this tune

before that summer? He made it up in that season and it stuck, that tall
young Christian African-American man
Bobby Root—another counselor—who called himself, however, only Root.

In those days it wasn't likely
that a guy like Root would know the first thing about how to shoot.
So when this advocate of peace, the sweetest, most beautiful and kindly

person I'd ever met, got later blown defenseless away
(so I imagine) in Vietnam: well, you wondered more than ever at the faith
that kept him keeping on, he claimed, both day and night,

that made him insist in song above the rope it was all right.

Girls in Their Upstairs Windows

Marcia Wrackham! Angelica Feuronig!
He never imagined a T-shirted boy like him,
Astride a pony (his own was named Miss Prim),
Would not again in a few scant decades coming

Be able to ride across their very lawns,
Would never get so breath-impairingly close.
Nor could he guess that pastures of green would cease
To claim their space. No, far beyond his ken,

The asphalt sealing the zones of his farthest dreams.
Suburban office parks, motels—a mall!
What's *that?* the kid might've wondered. What's a mall?
Back then each hill and wrangled hedgerow steamed.

He called it love, and maybe it was or wasn't.
How else, however, describe those urgent hours,
Based on Sunday's funnies though they were,
With sighs by "Brenda Starr" and others, the dozens

Of twilit rides till his loved ones left for college?
No matter the weather, he'd travel to visit them where—
Out of their windows—Elvis's "Teddy Bear"
On its 45 played their priviness to a knowledge

That he could surmise at fourteen, but hadn't quite caught.
Which meant he'd suffer their jokes: *Fat boy, fat horse!*
He'd defend Miss Prim, if not himself, of course;
For himself, he'd take their worst. So long as they'd talk.

Angie lived on the ridge, and Marcia a mile
To her north. He'd showily quirt his torpid pony
Like Mix or Gibson—matinee-idol cowboys—
Toward the ironies of each one's steely smile.

His affliction was one those heartthrobs recognized,
Both being belles, as used to be said, of the ball.
They spoke, come summer's end, from above it all,
Whenever they'd deign to speak, both much amused

To think that darkness would soon encumber the path
He'd have to travel homeward, the school day looming
—In all its literalness—for him next morning.
They were twinned in understanding he'd visit them both

Before he shooed Miss Prim to her stall and fed her,
Before he whipped his mind to the Monday assignment.
So he hated them some, for he couldn't know their amusement
Would seem a trivial torment decades later:

Angie has died, and Marcia's a wife-beater's hobby.
Or so he hears, having spoken to neither since then.
(By now the difference in ages would seem blade-thin.)
Into his memory swims the final Sunday

Visit to Marcia, Angie already gone.
After which, though night hastened down on the two
(Miss Prim and him, the steadiest belle and beau),
He squandered the very last of afternoon sun,

Dismounting, carving a crude heart into a beech,
Then knifing, with indiscriminate passion, *AF/*
MW, & (anonymous) *MYSELF.*
Soon, like surf, the confounding evening breached

His saddle's pommel. He shivered. Ahead remained
The treacherous creek to ford, and the witchy little
"Colored" graveyard to pass, with its tree-hung bottles,
Which the wind would always jangle. How to explain

Why he'd think then of village toughs, their jackets of leather
With their gaudy dragons, their mystic word, *KOREA?*
(Young brothers, he figures now, of guys in "the theater.")
He hoped that neither A nor M had encountered

Such guys, or "rocks," as we called them. He couldn't compete,
He and his hay-belly nag, with men so composed.
All of which was nonsense, he now can suppose,
Blessed as he is these days with a life complete

Without those girls, without the hideous pain
The real GIs must have suffered in Asian cold,
Where all they'd need were T-shirts, they'd been told. . . .
A life so mild that, despite a gentle rain,

His two youngest daughters can race across the lawn
To swim in their pond, while their father scribbles a poem,
One that—despite the evident blessings—leans
On other dreams that fell all over him.

Ballad

Near the art gallery basement, with its dark studios,
the building ensorceled by thick ivy vines;
near the gray granite mansion, august and ridiculous,

housing the spooks' club they called Skull and Bones;
X came down High Street one way, just as I
swaggered to meet him, headed the other;

I imagined *High Noon,* melodramatically
(myself some young Ivy League Gary Cooper).
Trouble loomed close, though what X had done

beforehand to turn me mysteriously mean
I've entirely forgotten. And now X is gone:
so notes the new issue of *Yale* magazine.

I figured that I was his equal, at least,
so felt more adrenalized than afraid,
and near disembodied on the quietened back street.

Yet I did mean to cave in the s.o.b.'s head.
No, not really—because this was just middle-class
confrontation: no weapons, no mayhem or murder.

We knew that such violence as might come to pass
relied (early sixties) on a prevalent order,
on rules and assumptions to which each was bound.

Life always surprises. I threw a wild right,
X blocked it and swung: I went heavily down.
He was lucky: hell, *he* didn't know how to fight

any more than I did; we were training as "leaders,"
though now I think too I was training to love
and to register breaks in the order, odd wonders:

the white constellations wheeling above
seemed spirits observing my brief minor pain;
and X's expression was gratified, yes,

yet also, by starlight and gaslight, benign.
So it seemed hard to tell who had won and who lost.
Both of our futures appeared well assured.

We shook hands, then we parted, like ghosts or like lovers,
slow-moving and sated, not breathing a word,
but now and then peering back over our shoulders,

as if what had happened held something worth saving . . .
which it must have. What was it? I couldn't have said,
though it strangely involved a spiritual seeing,

which lingers—or does it?—now that poor X is dead.

Ars Longa, Vita Brevis

—Grand Lake Stream, 1998

Sure. But isn't it *vita* that we want?
King Lear, most might agree, is a masterpiece,
but the author a mote in God's eye. Like anyone.
I'd love to meet good Geoffrey face to face,
maybe even invite him down to camp,
beside these falls. We'd broil a steak on the fire,
enjoy a couple of ales, maybe tell some tales.

I had no reason to plant that damned thing here
—white pine among exactly identical pines—
back thirty years, above the streamside ledge,
with its Passamaquoddy petroglyph of the sun,
beneath which lopes a handsome, close-coupled buck.
No motive now but sentiment to mourn
the tree's ruined top, which bodes its imminent drop

into the rapids. But I'm a sentimental
sort, and always was. There on the ledge,
one SUZI has also shallowly carved her name
and the year of her violation: '96.
Her chisel will never prove strong enough, however,
to stand the test of weather, her lack of will
so unlike the aboriginal carver's ardor.

His deer and planet have stayed these centuries.
Do people still take heart from Bishop's "One Art"?

Do people still attend to what manner of woman
great Dickinson was? We mutter clichés about her
famous dress, say, colored like a shirt
recently found over east, on the Slattery Road,
the garment's owner missing, it seems, forever.

A week, that is. The hounds couldn't keep his vanishing
scent in summer heat as he ploughed the blackswamp,
where by now he has foundered. Or maybe he's somewhere else,
with a brand new life, chuckling over the story
that the press and TV carry. Chuckling for now.
The local station has shown a picture or two
by his hand—tear-jerkers: he dabbled in watercolors.

I wonder where SUZI is? My pines stay thick:
not likely as thick as that awful swamp's vegetation,
but enough I'll have to chop a few to see
the stream again. (Flow gently till I end . . .)
I'll get to that. If she'd labored to cut in deeper,
then maybe, after half a millennium,
like me, somebody might kneel down on this stone

and marvel at SUZI's inarticulate sign,
which she meant nonetheless as lasting testimony,
like the Native American's rampant beast and sunshine.
The lost or dead man came from Massachussetts;
his father's a fellow with serious heart disease,
who for all of that has made his heartsick trip
way up this way because for seven days

he helplessly clung to the phone, his son having "none
of a woodsman's skills." The local weekly paper
displays some paintings too. They're not half bad.
Too bad the state has ended its useless search,

though Passamaquoddy officials—because this trouble
presented itself within their township—plan
to take it over, to find the artist, whatever

the find will amount to: a sad clan's trek to a church
he quit early on and then to a family plot.
And after many a summer dies the swan.
Like eponymous SUZI. The Passamaquoddys will show
their comfort in countryside that brought him down.
Crane jumped. Or fell. And what of Randall Jarrell?
The Indians' ease is not unlike the ease

of the buck that the skillful carver rendered in stone,
ten yards from my window, near which, despite its ruin,
my planted pine still leans, its remaining needles
the amber of tannin, its trunk completely lichened,
like the marker at great Coleridge's Highgate grave.
Oh, what I'd give for a chat with Red Warren again!
For women and men, like rock, to hold their stands.

Authority

—for WDW, who wrote North of Now

The times were good for him back thirty years;
he must have thought he'd risen above us all,
But they went more than well for the rest of us as well.
Chick's in those times was Topsfield's only store

and pumped the only gas for miles. The trucks
filled up the lot like milling pachyderms.
Back then of course we thought in different terms:
we never dreamed, say, Chick would have that stroke.

The pumps—all gone. Across the road, the Mobil-
Mart shows antiseptic, moony-white.
The traitor loggers lunch there day and night,
gaze through breath-gauzed glass, and watch *Chick's* crumble.

A river drew us friends together: trout,
in water clear as air. The trout have vanished,
along with some of us. Chick had a flourish
whenever he'd greet our gang. All grins and shouts.

He forgets who we are or else he doesn't care—
just aging guys from a state away, who come
for a bag of chips, for a rusted tin of ham,
for old times' sake. We wander through the store,

buying whatever we can, which isn't much.
Chick's locked in study, cards on the table, locked
in silence too, who above all things would talk
our very ears off when we stopped for lunch.

For tasty lunch: the poachers' moose were thick:
he could make himself a killing on steaks and burgers.
He'd wave his flipper and rant on local matters
(though he never let the meat get overcooked):

taxes, timber, a surefire fishing hole.
His face would shine with pure authority,
a different thing from this solemnity.
He'd hoot, opine; opine again, and smile.

Everything tends toward wisdom. Chick's dumb version
looks as grim as ever grim could be.
Friends at his table, he in better days,
the fish, the food: was all of that mere vision?

Outside, we recall how we dubbed him "Mr. Mayor."
And that's what he seemed, that stiff at his solitaire.
Full above our river, the moon appears
authoritative. Grins from ear to ear.

Fin de Siècle

I'm on The Lookout, as our family long ago named it.
   From this lichen-shawled moraine, the locally famous
      Connecticut River oxbow allows itself to be seen
         As well as from anywhere. Again and again
            I go on The Lookout, the view by now so familiar

It seems eternal, which makes me (though I know better)
   Think of myself up here as eternal too.
      We're supposed to be having spring, but this morning a mantle of snow
         Lingers on ledges, and even downhill to the south,
            The grass sulks underground around the house.

Indoors, our daughter, nine, is playing the New
   World symphony on her lately refurbished piano.
      This morning the vet phoned to say poor Pancho had died,
         The cat who'd been ours for nearly two decades.
            Dvorak's air can stab a susceptible heart

Even on better days. "New world," new start.
   I don't much care for cats, but I cared for that one:
      He suffered all that torment from all five normal children
         Without a scratch and—pardon my fallacy—
            Appeared to encounter death with dignity.

Made sure before moving, say, that his hindmost parts
   Were beneath him, as well as they *could* be. The melody starts

Again, again, again. How well Catherine plays, her future
　　Before her, bright prospect, despite this millennial weather,
　　　　These May Day snows. Far down: a stretch of river

In which—as we rode to school the week before last—
　　Lay a patch of open water she called The Gash.
　　　　(A curious family habit, yes, this giving of names.)
　　　　　　There's also a rock she calls Wise Arab upstream.
　　　　　　That Arab can tell how a day will develop: fine

As a rule, at worst a mixture of cloud and sun.
　　She said The Gash was "the place where everything comes,"
　　　　By which it seemed she meant each thought, or feeling, or dream.
　　　　　　I wonder where she fetches these notions of hers;
　　　　　　　　But in any case the Gash has disappeared,

Despite the cold. I'm glad. It hurt to imagine
　　—as somehow I did—that our spirits' products vanish
　　　　Into such black and fluid and fatal fridigity.
　　　　　　Just now, her tears must splash on the ice-white keys.
　　　　　　　　From The Lookout I inwardly see them, although I've claimed

　　　　That the place is eternal, above all change and pain.
　　　　And claim so still, in need of hopeful refrain.

Champlain: West Shore: Cartesian

Three decades have flown, but that's where Evvie's camp burned down.
There, the ledge, swept bare, on which my brother, who's gone, and I leaned,
tridents in hand. Perch, rock bass rose upward to our crumbs—the "plan"—
then we'd thrust and gig them. Up they came, flip-flopping, their pain a thing
we never once considered. There's the house where Uncle Dean and Emelda,
the farm wife, had their famous wager: Dean got through her cellar window,
Emelda caught herself midpoint. How could it happen? She was fat, no doubt,
but Dean an elephant. Today I think it must have had to do with class: he was
a broker, lived in the city; she was hard-working country, she was an iron-ass,

and muscle doesn't give. We telephoned the fire department. She's still alive,
I think. Therefore she is. For mind, it mustn't give. I flunked philosophy. I
couldn't remember a thing, just little bits and snatches, still don't think I can.
The beach was all gravel patches. Asphalt now. And yet its stones were hard
enough to kill my pet crow. Today a madman shot Yitzhak Rabin. The ferry
hasn't changed that much. What to think of Yasser Arafat? Don't burden me
with questions. God, but Uncle Dean was fat. The crow had a broken left wing
(a dog caught him roaming). He fell from his branch because he couldn't fly:
the bandage. The memory stings. But this isn't myth. This isn't that Icarus I

only recall from a painting. *Ticonderoga,* gorgeous paddle wheeler, once plied
these very waters. She's in a museum, across the lake on the eastern shore.
The ferry goes the other way. Oh, I loved her barbershop, her bar, all mirrors,
I think. Therefore they were. In the museum are works by Ogden Pleissner,
best gun-dog artist ever. (He hated to hunt with a dog.) We all are on our way
to visit my cousin, Uncle Dean's real nephew, and my first childhood hero. My
cousin must be sixty. God! I think. Therefore he is. Yes, the oak-framed

mirrors. Yes, the smell of summer, hot stones, and lake waves' rote. Back there,
I think, is where poor Evvie's camp burned down. I made love here, in a boat,

a dory: it was our first, and quite bad. Years later I heard that the woman had
a stroke. Or girl, if I'm to speak precisely. I was, to quote old books, a lad.
She's still a girl in mind, and I, in every sense, a boy—one whose mind is not
full of joy but shame. I should have seen my cousin before three decades
came and went. And why not phone that poor girl, be at the funeral (I mean
the uncle's)? What have I been thinking for all these years? I'm fifty-three.
Right there, the Syrup River—see? We'd shoot its frogs, who would quiver
by their pads. Why doesn't this bring tears? We'd fry them up for supper,
legs kicking in the pan. Who in hell was Evvie? What did *I* know? Back then

I could not care, nor care for the perch or rock bass, whose pale fillets, also,
got fried in the same big skillet. She wasn't by God a broker. It *was* a "camp,"
after all. I still can by God skin any fish like a champ. Even some great socker.
I didn't notice, really, the oaken bar, the barbershop with mirrors. So now,
you see, I do—as if I were looking in them—but all these years have fled
since then; I have no choice but to say: *Hell, I was only a kid.* Who was Evvie,
I wonder? Everything to me was like a rumor. There her place burned down.
All I knew was that it did. I remember '67, fifteen years later. Was it then
Rabin was the hero? And what after all is a hero? For God's sake say, explain.

Twenty-five miles northeast is a *hamlet* named South Hero. Well. A fellow,
by the time he's fifty-three, ought to know some things. Over there we'd fling
our lures when we got older. My brother. Me. Smallmouths broke our leaders,
often as not, God bless them, and got away. And my children . . . I try to explain
to my children. They clamor for explanation, I think. Therefore they do. I try
to explain that Evvie lived out there on the the point. And that her place
burned down. And that a person should learn, too, and should hold that
learning in mind, as if it were muscle, or there's no world to explore, explain:
No point. No Emelda. No Dean. No gleaming steamboat. No frog or fish or crow.

No ruinous flame. No philosophy (to call it so). No thought. . . . No now but pain.

Wife-Tracking

Men and women follow different rhythms.
No, more than merely different: poles apart,
According to the age's trendy wisdoms.

Perhaps sometimes she feels an actual start;
Looking up from her desk, she may be stunned
By the sky of middle February, blue

That's so much more than blue, and unruly sun
That lays a string of gems on the aging snow.
Upon which, work be damned, she climbs our ridge.

And sometimes I myself, some hours later,
Can cease my maundering over a stubborn page.
Sun will have traveled ever so much farther

Down than I'd have dreamed. So up I get
From my own desk. I crack the study door,
And even though my hearing is a wreck,

My ears perceive the ravens' repertoire
In all its wild variety: that bleat,
That audible yawn, that scold, that cheep, that bawl.

I take to the ridge, upon whose sheet the feet
Of that same lissome wife have earlier scrawled
A furtive script I seek to understand.

I follow the vanishing trail, eyes down, intent,
Some story meanwhile scripting itself in mind.
I also imagine I catch a mixture of scents:

Like a working hound, I chuff and snuff, discerning
Fresh air, shampoo, wet wool, some human musk.
The story's a mixture too—of sadness, yearning.

I circle back to the new-lit house. It's dusk.
Perhaps inside I'll sense those scents for certain.
There are times when disparate rhythms coalesce.

I see her penumbral shape behind a curtain.
There's more than I deserve in this life of bliss.

What He Knows

At 3 A.M. each night, or more accurately, morning, he awakes and reads
Authors whose beautiful skill both soothes and makes him sleepless.

Praise genius! he thinks, then feels, in his state as minor author,
Stomach wrinkle like a butternut's case in October, which sensation is proof

Of almost unendurable horror, but which, likewise, bears witness
(Look at that very savvy simile!) to what he knows, to what most don't:

How to set a 110 Conibear trap, the thought of which now, at fifty-six,
Chills the blood, the poor prey drowned. Gone underwater. Down . . .

The floret of the hop-hornbeam, which unchills that blood, which floret
Lasts through the winter, and on which feed the grouse, the hare, the . . .

Three ways in which to determine if a grouse is cock or hen . . .
The flight-signs in gloaming that say: Puddle-duck, not diving . . .

How, south and north in the east, unsung, black-and-white
Missionless experts, at risk to life and limb, wrought railroad ties:

With a sleeper ax, crude and deadly as the yeoman's battle-ax,
From which it was derived (check your heraldry) . . .

What a "cowcatcher" looked like, and why . . .
The click/hum mating song of the male whip-poor-will,

Who is on the point of whistling himself into memory while you go skiing,
You shits, you "lovers" of "outdoors," the while your snow-makers drown

All night the blessed coyotes' palaver, drown, drown . . .
Where a raven likes to nest . . .

The generous, warning handstand of the skunk that warns,
Back off, you worse-than-skunk . . .

O no, none of this knowledge, he'll allow, is of itelf meritorious.
O no, this is no more than *apologia pro vita sua.*

No, it's *pro vita mea.* It doesn't, shouldn't, earn me particular fame.
I just like the life of which each last detail is eloquent:

How to hunt bleak Codfish Ridge in the rain and, once there,
How wonder, though inland far we be, how it could get such a name . . .

How to get from Codfish to Pickledish without driving on tar,
And thence to Bingo, and next to that beechy sidehill in Linneus . . .

How to cook a pickerel so not a Y-bone's left in its succulent flesh . . .
How to jig through the ice for whitefish, then cook the whitefish too

(Same way, the clouds screaming, by noontime, over the bobhouse,
Whose stove spits fat, from up there by Porcupine Mountain) . . .

How and where to see the springtail, the "snow flea,"
As the snow gets corny, as the last of the old-time sugar makers hitches up

The last of the old-time working Belgians,
Blond and vast and beautiful . . .

How everything, I'm determined, can be beautiful, even when I'm up
At 3 A.M. As the real writers will insist, Still beautiful.

Part 4
Phases

Phases

—in praise of Zoloft

Where had the moon gone, slivered, halved, or full? Where indeed at all?

Eclipsed, you'd say. Praise, then, for what enabled me, enables me
    to sleep sometimes past 3 A.M., sky moon-soaked or moonless.
        Before, on waking, I'd feel quotidian annoyance segue
            straight to terror: I'd see one of our children stray careless

Onto pavement, say, and be stricken by a log-truck, tandem, longlog-laden,
    or the child's mother otherwise stricken, who in fact flourishes
        in optimum health, who remains mother of all mothers or lovers
            on earth, who marks all points on this my compass.

I can now fetch to my nose our aged neighbor's heirloom bloom of rose,
    my fingers eluding its stem thorns, such that I joy in its frail odor.
        I am put once more and lively too into the huntsman's field
            behind my chesty, breath-robbing, athlete pointer,

And put at this archaic machine, so that I witness what I have seen.
    Praise Zoloft, bringing back not only moon but also ambient woods
        and bird sound, such as the nesting raven's cluck-cry
            today, which for guests I identified, happy I hadn't forgot.

One pill a day regives, in brief, a nerve that once governed this my life,
    so that I don't sit fat in the fat corner chair in dull regard of limbs
        refusing to move, nor willfully stop the lift of these eyes
            when firstest brisk wind of firstest autumn slams

Hard down on the pond, the ragged white pine hedge, while just overhead
   a fish hawk hen fights hard to gather yards of hurtled air and then
      plunges entirely and thrillingly true to her target in water
         —trout or dace—with a fractional adjustment of wing,

Oh miracle! I'm inclined to face the moons, by way of inscrutable chemical,
   or other lights, like the one that kindles from that horse-mule's hide
      down by Cuthbertsons' barn, and can care now thus to be able.
         And I can care and weep for the local boy who lately died

Hard by his barn in a car, just then noticing perhaps same lucence pouring
   from same beast's flank. And I can care for another boy I love,
      who strays, strays—drugs/alchohol—and can grind my teeth
         because in me resides on this earth no power to save

Him nor a next. Still, however, I'm here, still give more than not a shit,
   And so offer praise for a concoction's dampening of other behaviors,
      whereby I have raced to settle things, whatever they were,
         to the point of hallucination, as if I were gripped by fever.

Hence praise, crude though it be, that I can at false dawn shit, precisely,
   and let such a thing finish itself in whatever time it may take,
      not bolt, having thumbed old magazines, uncomprehending,
         sure as I was that this waste suggested in fact the waste

Of existence. Praise that in playing one-on-one against our younger son,
   I can be not too grimly intent, as if life hung on a basket, a victory,
      that I can yet play hard and be beaten, nor always fear
         for that life, nor fear that by exertion I'll be

Fallen on the concrete slab, the son beside me, mystified and, I trust, sad.
   O praise that I now invite our youngest daughter, gleeful, to dive
      from my shoulders into that spring-fed pond without thinking
         withal and *instanter* how temporarily one lingers alive

And how they won't be squared, those shoulders, in a box to go under
    this ledgy earth but instead be among my embers, cast into Big Falls
        at my direction to fly seaward by way of Grand Lake Stream
            and then of the St. Croix River, where migrant eels

Will swim all through them, in the hunter's-moon dazzle of high autumn.
    I give thanks that before then I'll roam with Belle, the pointer,
        reading in October's hysterical leaves not imminent hell
            nor retribution for—small as they might seem to others—

My misfeasances as this father, this brother, child, importunate lover.
    Thanks be that I may consider with something akin to affection
        the snapping turtles who drown the black duck hatchlings
            here each year and be fond of them as clearers of carrion,

As I too may be, and surely was, by metaphor, up until this unsettling cure,
    unsettling for causing me to ponder hard its contradictions
        of my callow ideologies, as for example that we are a nation
            too disposed to pharmacological solutions,

Written by virtue of our inanities, our hundred hundred psychologies:
    E.g., that the condition of being child means a boy or girl must suffer
        from "attention deficit disorder." Prescriptions accrue
            by the same many hundred. For such reasons do I suffer

Mild despond, this being, sure as any of our small lives, a drug that I'm on,
    to which my brilliant wife suggests that I might have, oh, diabetes,
        and that I would not in that case refuse the insulin.
            Yet there exists, I believe, a larger issue—which teaches

Me perforce to meditate on these my means of escaping a personal fate
    derived, it seems, from biology, which—because of those means—
        I'm free to cheat: for this Zoloft, it costs. Oh God, it does cost.
            Thus what of those neighbors who are so strictly enchained

By debt, who have so many more motives for depression, and yet
     who must rise, before I daily do, to labor in mill-road-factory-field?
          Praise be, I guess, that though I go not into deeper despond
               (which never has helped anyone), I do still cling to guilt,

In that there exist too many distresses that have gone too long unaddressed,
     not that I am the one to address any—not any!—but that all must
          be studied. In that guilt keeps alive in me the American,
               which in perfectability may put too much of its trust,

Even by improvisation: thus in this season have I blessed the poor garden
     our family made in moonless June, June of the record-heavy storms,
          which all but undid the century-old library's foundation
               one town south, by which we may all be warned

Of nullifications caused by all us humans; and yet I can bless those ruins
     of garden, and even the same rains, greening our hills all August.
          I bless the summer, even unto its fragile worrisome moths
               that pipped and bumbled against our tent's canvas

And brushed my face in their dopey fatal tumbles through its small space,
     within which my family's breaths made small sweet wetness on air.
          O drug, help me bless the dog asleep on her mat at my feet—
               her jowls puffing and luffing as in her dream appears

Grouse after grouse, exploding from brush in that indescribable rush
     that I've seen all these years—as I bless you, suspicionable drug,
          which has turned my voice's commands to mild and apparent,
               such that the younger, green-broke dog

Comes to heel with apparent pleasure and does not bolt in terror
     from the unaccountable rage of the bad dog's handler
          (or rather the dog's bad handler), which now forces to mind
               my fits of rage at my dead father

When I was an adolescent child, a father who, more than merely mild,
 would wait out such storms with benignest expression,
  after which rant I contemplated, as if through thin glass,
   a world *arranged,* that is, stopped in strange procession:

In moonlight shone weirdly lawns and flowers, fences, lanes and pastures,
 so that I'd later see a great aptitude in a line from a great poem
  (would feel it shocked on the morrow of the father's perishing):
   "After great pain," said She, "a Formal—Feeling comes."

Praise be that Zoloft's alchemy enlists me again to listen to Nat Adderley
 on cornet, above all his opening lick on Buddha Monk's "Misterioso,"
  when Nat was playing for JJ, which was arguably the greatest
   —in the history of great brass jazz—ever solo intro.

Not that I would make strong any case against the nonpareil Armstrong, nor
 Miles, nor Diz, nor Clark, nor Freddie, than whom Nat himself
  would likely announce himself inferior, but that
   this is a side one must put on that special shelf

Of what-needs-to-be-played-played. So why think back on a revelatory day
 when I hooked my first trophy trout? I do not instantly think *loss*
  in either case, but that I have been a man much rewarded:
   fish; family; great classic permutations of low-down blues.

I had a feisty white grandpa, who knew not one bar of them blues, but who
 chased and whacked with an umbrella a trolleyman
  who hadn't stopped, for all that Grandpa was almost
   seventy. Grandpa, after, dropped down of an infarction

In the smokestack main street rain. There looked to be, in rapids, a stain
 —as on a senseless murderer's victim's—on the rainbow's gill-plate
  so that at first I misprised him for a native cutthroat,
   and, though that Montana river was in full spate,

When I came to the black ravine where I could not keep walking
    after that gorgeous creature, in odd faith I dove into whitest water
        and swam after the prey, rod in hand, till at length I was able
            to set my feet on the long blond sandbar, then slaughter

The beached fish by beating it on rock, and so could again stand and suck
    human air. Oh, I ought rather to have acknowledged the pull
        of saving current and let it go. I didn't know him. Still I picture
            my mad paternal kinsman, acting once more the fool,

Expiring, unwilling to be thought the fool. I can imagine him pining,
    some passerby on the sidewalk rebuking the driver of the tram:
        "For god's sake leave him in peace, leave him alone!
            Can't you see he's an old man?"

Never give up is my motto, as it was his, though life can come to this:
    Give up, it's going away, which going I've known at the least since
        a first panic attack at blue Yale, when the rescue squadmen
            bore me downstairs, five flights, past the famous fence.

And later, as on a gurney I lay spent, the while a Mississippi-slow resident
    took sweet time getting to me—dumb, seventeen—then asked,
        "Have you ever been in trouble with the law?" And I answered:
            "Doc, this heart is having what I think may be an attack.

"What'll you do, you son of a bitch, lift my driver's license?" At which
    he left. In the end (no end of course at all), I turned out to show
        —by way of No-Doz and innumerable cups of coffee—a huge
            adrenaline count, having vigiled four full days now

On texts that, all semester I should have been reading, rather than playing
    pool, at which I became good enough that I and good Bart Weldt
        hustled our way through that good-good trip to Key West
            one spring. Now Bart is still as any damned dead smelt.

Where am I heading? Maybe to where, for example, that trout-devouring
        otter who ravaged the pond on this past Thanksgiving Day
                becomes not so much thief or nuisance as the purest marvel
                        (as indeed she is, or he), of whose predation I now say:

It reconfirms assuredness that in a world there can be surety, blessedness,
        and that I can find myself blessed in other random daily matters,
                as, say, that my aged Ford truck did pull me the full way home
                        last night, deferring the death of its alternator

Until I pulled into our driveway, midnight, took the stairs, lit the hall light,
        looked in on the sleeping children, each of whom I kissed,
                and then on my wife, who waved a languid hand and fell back,
                        then I took a cigar to the lawn, looked back at our house

As over it, up from Mt. Moosilauke's westmost knoll, a moon climbed full,
        and rather than, as once, seeing at once all in the world that is brief
                in such resplendent form, I surmised, by drug or God or both,
                        how it all might at last in fact come round—this my life.

And I vowed to wander, in proper wonder, a valley of the shadow of death.

Illinois Poetry Series
Laurence Lieberman, Editor

History Is Your Own Heartbeat
Michael S. Harper (1971)

The Foreclosure
Richard Emil Braun (1972)

The Scrawny Sonnets and Other
   Narratives
Robert Bagg (1973)

The Creation Frame
Phyllis Thompson (1973)

To All Appearances: Poems New and
   Selected
Josephine Miles (1974)

The Black Hawk Songs
Michael Borich (1975)

Nightmare Begins Responsibility
Michael S. Harper (1975)

The Wichita Poems
Michael Van Walleghen (1975)

Images of Kin: New and Selected Poems
Michael S. Harper (1977)

Poems of the Two Worlds
Frederick Morgan (1977)

Cumberland Station
Dave Smith (1977)

Tracking
Virginia R. Terris (1977)

Riversongs
Michael Anania (1978)

On Earth as It Is
Dan Masterson (1978)

Coming to Terms
Josephine Miles (1979)

Death Mother and Other Poems
Frederick Morgan (1979)

Goshawk, Antelope
Dave Smith (1979)

Local Men
James Whitehead (1979)

Searching the Drowned Man
Sydney Lea (1980)

With Akhmatova at the Black Gates
Stephen Berg (1981)

Dream Flights
Dave Smith (1981)

More Trouble with the Obvious
Michael Van Walleghen (1981)

The American Book of the Dead
Jim Barnes (1982)

The Floating Candles
Sydney Lea (1982)

Northbook
Frederick Morgan (1982)

Collected Poems, 1930–83
Josephine Miles (1983; reissue, 1999)

The River Painter
Emily Grosholz (1984)

Healing Song for the Inner Ear
Michael S. Harper (1984)

The Passion of the Right-Angled Man
T. R. Hummer (1984)

The Ways We Touch
Miller Williams (1997)

The Rooster Mask
Henry Hart (1998)

The Trouble-Making Finch
Len Roberts (1998)

Grazing
Ira Sadoff (1998)

Turn Thanks
Lorna Goodison (1999)

Traveling Light: Collected and New Poems
David Wagoner (1999)

Some Jazz a While: Collected Poems
Miller Williams (1999)

The Iron City
John Bensko (2000)

Songlines in Michaeltree: New and
Collected Poems
Michael S. Harper (2000)

Pursuit of a Wound
Sydney Lea (2000)

The Pebble: Old and New Poems
Mairi MacInnes (2000)

National Poetry Series

Eroding Witness
Nathaniel Mackey (1985)
Selected by Michael S. Harper

Palladium
Alice Fulton (1986)
Selected by Mark Strand

Cities in Motion
Sylvia Moss (1987)
Selected by Derek Walcott

The Hand of God and a Few Bright
Flowers
William Olsen (1988)
Selected by David Wagoner

The Great Bird of Love
Paul Zimmer (1989)
Selected by William Stafford

Stubborn
Roland Flint (1990)
Selected by Dave Smith

The Surface
Laura Mullen (1991)
Selected by C. K. Williams

The Dig
Lynn Emanuel (1992)
Selected by Gerald Stern

My Alexandria
Mark Doty (1993)
Selected by Philip Levine

The High Road to Taos
Martin Edmunds (1994)
Selected by Donald Hall

Theater of Animals
Samn Stockwell (1995)
Selected by Louise Glück

The Broken World
Marcus Cafagña (1996)
Selected by Yusef Komunyakaa

Nine Skies
A. V. Christie (1997)
Selected by Sandra McPherson

Lost Wax
Heather Ramsdell (1998)
Selected by James Tate

So Often the Pitcher Goes to Water until
  It Breaks
Rigoberto González (1999)
Selected by Ai

Other Poetry Volumes

Local Men and *Domains*
James Whitehead (1987)

Her Soul beneath the Bone: Women's
  Poetry on Breast Cancer
Edited by Leatrice Lifshitz (1988)

Days from a Dream Almanac
Dennis Tedlock (1990)

Working Classics: Poems on Industrial
  Life
*Edited by Peter Oresick and Nicholas
  Coles* (1990)

Hummers, Knucklers, and Slow Curves:
  Contemporary Baseball Poems
Edited by Don Johnson (1991)

The Double Reckoning of Christopher
  Columbus
Barbara Helfgott Hyett (1992)

Selected Poems
Jean Garrigue (1992)

New and Selected Poems, 1962–92
Laurence Lieberman (1993)

The Dig and *Hotel Fiesta*
Lynn Emanuel (1994)

For a Living: The Poetry of Work
*Edited by Nicholas Coles and Peter
  Oresick* (1995)

The Tracks We Leave: Poems on
  Endangered Wildlife of North America
Barbara Helfgott Hyett (1996)

Peasants Wake for Fellini's *Casanova* and
  Other Poems
*Andrea Zanzotto; edited and translated by
  John P. Welle and Ruth Feldman;
  drawings by Federico Fellini and
  Augusto Murer* (1997)

Moon in a Mason Jar and *What My Father
  Believed*
Robert Wrigley (1997)

The Wild Card: Selected Poems, Early
  and Late
*Karl Shapiro; edited by Stanley Kunitz and
  David Ignatow* (1998)

Turtle, Swan and *Bethlehem in Broad
  Daylight*
Mark Doty (2000)

Typeset in 9.5/14 Usherwood
with Moonshine display
Designed by Paula Newcomb
Composed by Jim Proefrock
at the University of Illinois Press
Manufactured by Cushing-Malloy, Inc.

University of Illinois Press
1325 South Oak Street
Champaign, IL 61820–6903
www.press.uillinois.edu